COOKING IN STYLE

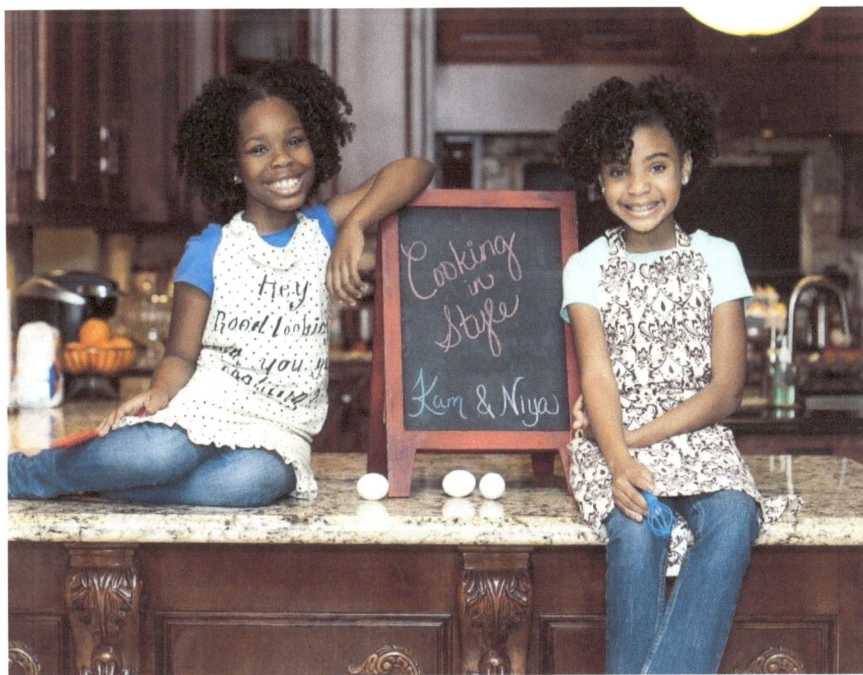

Authored and Illustrated by:

Kamryn Johnson & Saniya Scott

Copyright

To order additional copies of this book, contact:
Kam & Niya

www.KamAndNiya.com

DEDICATON

This book is dedicated to our parents, grandparents, family, teachers, and friends. Thanks for your love, prayers, and support. We love you all!

FOREWORD
BY CHEF EDDIE JACKSON

"Everyone has the ability to be their own personal chef! "
- Chef Eddie Jackson

Master Chef, Season 4
The Next Food Network Star, Season 11
Caribbean Grill, Owner
Fit Chef Gym, Owner
Food Network BBQ Blitz

I am extremely passionate about cooking, as I believe that nothing brings people together better than a great meal. Food is a universal language and although preparation and ingredients vary from culture to culture, the dynamic remains the same. Cooking is an art, and we all have the ability to create. Cooking is very humbling. It takes patience, care, and a slight level of discernment. As a chef, it is beyond rewarding when I am able to create a meal that changes someone's day for the better. I encourage everyone young & old to become comfortable navigating around the kitchen. I am extremely enthused to know that Kamryn and Saniya are demonstrating that cooking can be fun at a young age. Not only does this book contain recipes, it contains healthy ingredient options along with stories that every child is sure to enjoy. I encourage all parents to set aside time each week to cook and read with their children. This is a great family activity and I believe that it will develop their appreciation for the art of cooking. "Cooking in Style" is a great beginner's cookbook for every child to find his or her inner chef.

Eddie Jackson

Contents & Recipes

INSTRUCTIONS

1. Be aware of any food allergies. Food recipes in this book may contain dairy, eggs, wheat, soybean, peanuts, tree nuts, fish, and shellfish. Substitute where necessary to avoid allergens.

2. Always read the entire recipe before beginning. This will help you prepare all ingredients and any necessary tools.

3. Rinse all fruit and vegetables thoroughly prior to using in all recipes.

4. Wash hands with anti-bacterial hand wash and warm water before handling food to make sure germs are not passed along.

5. Think Safety: Pull back hair out of sight so it doesn't get into food.

6. Wear apron, if necessary, to protect clothes.

7. Ask an adult for assistance when using the oven, stovetop, or appliances. An adult should always be present while appliances are in use.

8. Ask questions: This is the best way to learn.

9. Have fun! Make the recipes your own. Add ingredients that you like and remove ingredients that you do not like. Be creative!

CONVERSION CHART
MEASUREMENTS & TEMPERATURES

CUP TO TABLESPOON TO TEASPOON TO MILLILITERS (CUP TO ML)

1 cup = 16 Tbsp = 48 tsp = 240 ml
3/4 cup = 12 Tbsp = 36 tsp = 180 ml
2/3 cup = 11 Tbsp = 32 tsp = 160 ml
1/2 cup = 8 Tbsp = 24 tsp = 120 ml
1/3 cup = 5 Tbsp = 16 tsp = 80 ml
1/4 cup = 4 Tbsp = 12 tsp = 60 ml
1 Tablespoon = 15 ml
1 teaspoon = 5 ml

CUP TO FLUID OUNCES (CUP TO FL. OZ)

1 cup = 8 fl oz
3/4 cup = 6 fl oz
2/3 cup = 5 fl oz
1/2 cup = 4 fl oz
1/3 cup = 3 fl oz
1/4 cup = 2 fl oz

FAHRENHEIT TO CELCIUS (F TO C)

500 F = 260 C
475 F = 245 C
450 F = 235 C
425 F = 220 C
400 F = 205 C
375 F = 190 C
350 F = 180 C
325 F = 160 C
300 F = 150 C
275 F = 135 C
250 F = 120 C
225 F = 107 C

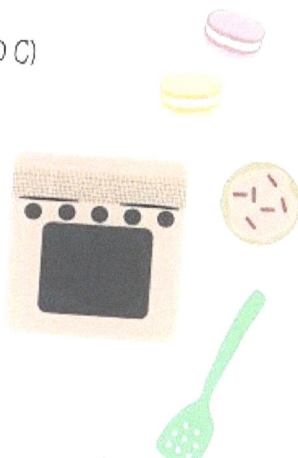

Kid Chefs just wanna have FUN!!

Breakfast

Don't Delay! It's the most important meal of the day!

Mommy's Helper

"Wake up Babygirl!! Mommy overslept so we need to rush and get dressed for work and school. I have an early morning meeting, and I absolutely cannot be late!"

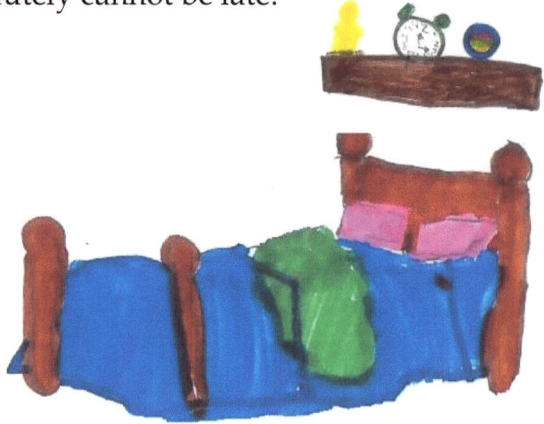

Skye hops out of bed and rushes into the bathroom to brush her teeth and to get dressed. She quickly makes up her bed and snatches up her backpack.

"Great, I beat my mom getting ready", Skye shouted. "My mommy is in a hurry and won't have time to eat breakfast. Maybe, I can help her out by making something quick and yummy. "Hmmm what can I fix?", Skye pondered. "I have the perfect idea! ", Skye shouted.

Skye goes to the cabinet and grabs a plastic cup. "Mommy

will be able to take her breakfast with her!!" Skye pulls out the

following ingredients:

- 2 Strawberries (Cut into ½ or ¼ slices)
- 2 Blueberries
- Greek Strawberry Yogurt (or favorite yogurt)
- Honey Granola (or favorite granola flavor)
- Honey

First, Skye grabs a cup and layers the bottom of the cup with

two tablespoons of yogurt. Skye covers the layer of yogurt

with granola. She continues to repeat her steps by layering

with yogurt and granola until she reaches the top of the cup.

Lastly, she neatly places the strawberries and blueberries on

top, and finishes the masterpiece off with a light drizzle of

honey.

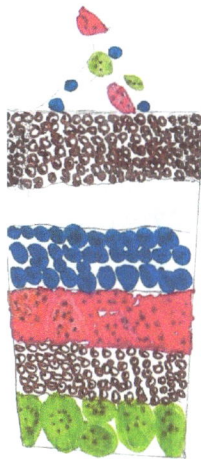

"Mom is going to love this", she thought. Skye's mom shouts sternly across the house,"Skye, I hope you are dressed and ready to leave!" Skye's mom gathers her briefcase, purse and keys and dashes into the kitchen where she was greeted by Skye holding up a Fruit and Yogurt parfait with a huge smile on her face. "Mom, I didn't want you to miss breakfast, and be hungry in your meeting. It is the most important meal of the day!

"Skye, I love you so much, and you are the sweetest daughter on earth. I can't wait to eat what you've made for me." Skye and her mom took their parfaits with them, and left to begin their day. Skye learned on this day to find small ways that she could help her mom, so that getting ready for school and work could be a tad bit easier.

Whole Grain Hot Chocolate Pancakes

Ingredients

- 2 cups whole grain pancake mix

- ¼ cup sugar

- 2 tablespoons baking cocoa

- 1 cup chocolate milk

- 1 teaspoon vanilla

- 2 eggs

Toppings (optional)

- Mini Marshmallows

- Chocolate Candy Sprinkles

- Chocolate-flavor Syrup

- Whipped Cream

Directions

1. In a large bowl, stir all ingredients, except toppings, with wire whisk until well blended. Heat nonstick griddle to 375°F or 12-inch skillet over medium-high heat. (To test

griddle, sprinkle with a few drops of water. If bubbles jump around, heat is just right.) Brush with vegetable oil or spray with cooking spray before heating.

2. For each pancake, pour approximately ¼ cup of batter on the hot griddle. Cook 2 to 3 minutes or until bubbly on top and dry around edges. Turn; cook other side until light golden brown around edges.

3. Drizzle pancakes with chocolate-flavor syrup; top with whipped cream. Sprinkle with marshmallows and chocolate candy sprinkles.

- Kids can cook too! Let your imagination run free until it becomes a recipe. -

Breakfast Muffins

Ingredients

- 4 Eggs

- Shredded Cheese

- Diced Meat of Choice: Bacon/Sausage/Turkey/Ham

Tools:

- Muffin Pan

- Cupcake Baking Cups

- Ladle

Directions:

1. Preheat oven to 350° F.

2. Place the baking cups in the muffin pan.

3. Beat eggs in a bowl.

4. Add meat and cheese.

5. Use a ladle to fill each baking cup ¾ full.

6. Bake for 15-18 minutes or until lightly browned.

Lunch

Munch…Munch… Munch on Lunch!

All Natural PB & J

Ingredients

- All natural peanut or almond butter
- Jelly (Grape)
- Whole wheat/grain bread

There were two friends, Kennedy and Nyla, who had playdates every other week together. One play date, Kennedy's mom took them to the park. When they got there, Kennedy's mom told the girls that they could go play, but make sure they stay together. They decided to go to the slide. When they climbed across the monkey bars to the slide, they found an alligator hiding inside. They asked nicely multiple times if he could move, but he stayed in the same spot the whole time, until a big breeze came by. Then the alligator slid out in front of the slide, and stood up. The children asked him again if he could move, but he just stood

there. Nyla said, "Maybe we can get him to move away with our all natural peanut butter jelly sandwiches. So Nyla and Kennedy told the alligator to do some vocal lessons, and in one of the lessons the alligator had to open his mouth. The girls quickly shoved the all-natural peanut butter jelly sandwich in the alligator's mouth! The PB and J had a potion that made animals and people start to be nice, and that is what the alligator did. He was nice and moved from the slide so Nyla and Kennedy could play. "Thank you so much" Nyla said to the alligator. An hour later the girls left and told their moms the whole story.

The Ultimate Snack Pack

Ingredients
- Ham or Turkey Rounds
- Sliced Cheese (cut in fours)
- Round Crackers
- Grapes
- Sugar free drink
- Water

Tools
- Baking cups
- 4 section Tupperware

Directions
1. Separate each ingredient in a cupcake baking cup.
2. Store in lunch Tupperware.

Hey, my name is Erin and I do not like the cafeteria food at my school. I really want them to have snack packs because those are my favorite. Instead, every day they have to have gross mashed potatoes, corn, and pizza.

"Can I have your attention please? From what was told to me, we are having a different lunch today but it will be a surprise for all of you!"

I could not believe what was said. I really hope we are having Snack Packs, but at least we are having a different lunch. But at least we are having a different lunch. Now I could not wait until lunch came!   (2 hours later)

Now it is lunch time, and everybody is excited to see what we are having! It's Snack Packs! I rushed to the line to see how everything was set up! There were lots of colorful cupcake baking cups filled with different kinds of meat and fruit for us to pick what we wanted in our Snack Packs. We even got to pick our drinks. I want them to have Snack Packs every Friday for lunch. We had so much fun making our own lunches! Erin finished her lunch, and when she got home, she told her mom all about lunch time. Erin made a request the next day at school to have Snack Packs for lunch every Friday, and the school said yes! Now Erin loves lunch at school! She started thinking of what else she could change in the cafeteria.

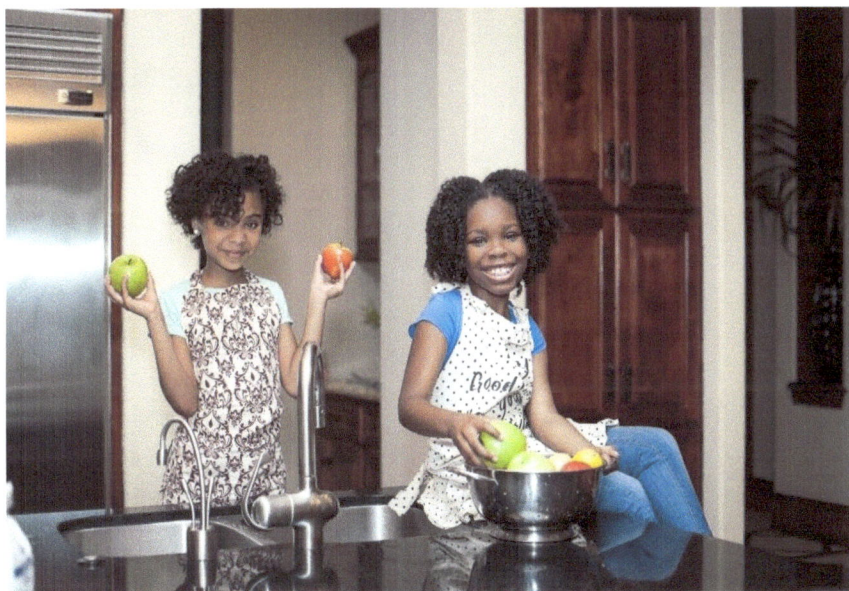

An **apple** a day,
keeps the
doctors away!

Snacks

When hunger ATTACKS, fix a SNACK!!!

Fresh Fruit Rainbow Ka-Bobs

Ingredients

- Sliced Strawberries
- Sliced Cantaloupe or Mandarin Oranges
- Pineapple Chunks
- Sliced Kiwi or Honey Dew Melon
- Fresh Blueberries
- Purple Grapes

Tools

- Wooden or Bamboo Skewers

Make sure all splinters are removed from skewers by rolling two together in your hands, or by rubbing them over each other. Ask parent/guardian for help with removing splinters.

Directions

1. Cut the fruit that is not already small into 1-inch, or bite-size, chunks.
2. First, skewer the strawberry.
3. Then, skewer the cantaloupe or orange.
4. Then, skewer the pineapple.
5. Then, skewer the kiwi or honey-dew melon.
6. Then, skewer the blueberries.
7. Lastly skewer the grapes.
8. Enjoy! Your Kabob should represent each color of the rainbow. ☺

Apple Smiles

Ingredients

- 1 Red Apple
- Miniature Marshmallows
- Peanut Butter or Caramel

Directions:

1. Slice apple into eighths.
2. Layer peanut butter or caramel topping on one side of the apple slice.
3. Place 4 marshmallows in between two slices. (The marshmallows should be placed on the coated sides of the apples.

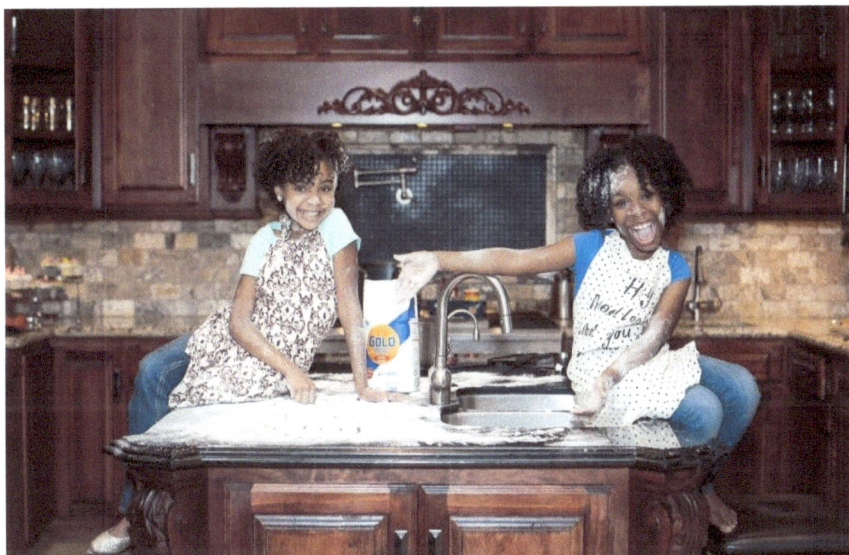

There is no such thing as a **MESS** in the kitchen!

Dinner
Time

Cooking with Grandma

"Today I get to spend the day with my granny. She is the nicest grownup on the planet, and I can't wait to see what she has planned for us", thought Symone. She always has fun treats and is as happy to see me as I am to see her.

Symone couldn't stop smiling just thinking of the possibilities of today.

"We're here", said Symone's mom as she left the driveway. Symone jumped out of the car, and ran to the front door where her grandma was waiting with open arms. They hugged and greeted each other before entering.

"Bye mom!! I love you", waved Symone.

Symone's mom waved goodbye as she backed out of the driveway.

"Oh, I have a surprise for you my precious granddaughter", said Grandma.

Symone couldn't wait. Last time she was at her grandma's

house they sewed aprons together, and the time before that, they made jewelry. Symone loved making crafts. "What is it grandma? I can't wait!" screeched Symone.

"Today, we are going to make Chicken & Shrimp Alfredo Pasta", said grandma.

"How does Grandma know that this is my favorite dish?" thought Symone. "She must be a mind reader because I am super hungry."

"Yay granny, let's get started", said Symone.

Ingredients:

- 1 - 16 oz. Can of Alfredo Sauce
- 10 oz. of Angel Hair Pasta Noodles
- 3 Chicken Breast
- 1 lb. of Shrimp
- 1 cap of Vegetable Oil
- 3 cups of mixed cheese
- ¼ teaspoon of Pepper for Chicken
- 1 teaspoon of Seasoned Salt for Chicken and Shrimp
- 2/3 cup of Butter for sautéed shrimp
- ½ teaspoon of chicken rub

Directions:

1. Cook the chicken on a grill or in skillet after seasoning with seasoning.
2. Season shrimp with seasoned salt and then sautee on stove with butter. Then add shrimp and butter and cook until shrimp starts to turn pink, just a few minutes.
3. Bring big pot of water to boil and cook pasta as directed. (Set pasta aside.)

4. In a separate pot, start cooking Alfredo sauce and slowly add cheese while stirring.

5. Once cheese is completely stirred into pasta, add chicken and shrimp into the pasta.

6. Pour sauce over noodles and ENJOY!

Strawberry & Spinach Salad

Ingredients

- 1 Pint of Fresh Strawberries (rinsed)
- 1 Package of Baby Spinach

Toppings

- Pecan Halve (optional)
- Vinaigrette Dressing
- Crumbled Feta cheese

Instructions

1. Remove tops from strawberries.

2. Slice strawberries into halves.

3. Use tongs to mix salad.

4. Add in pecan halves and feta cheese, if desired.

5. Top with dressing per serving.

Beauty and the Burger

Ingredients

- 1 lb. Ground Turkey
- Whole Grain Burger buns
- Seasoned Salt
- Condiments (optional)
    - Mustard
    - Mayo
    - Pickles
    - Lettuce
    - Tomatoes
    - Cheese
    - Ketchup

Directions:

1. Moderately season ground turkey with seasoned salt.
2. Roll a handful of meat into balls, and smash into burger patties.
3. Brown the patties in a skillet (medium heat) until no longer pink inside.
4. Add toppings and serve!

Today is my birthday which means a big party, fancy dresses, and fancy foods. I hate birthdays. I just want to hang with my friends outside the palace, and do regular kid stuff. Every year, my parents hire caterers to serve these outrageous foods that I can't even pronounce. Can I just have pizza or French fries or a burger? I really want to try burgers because eating fancy foods all the time is making me sick! Oh well, it's time to get dressed now.

The music is playing and the guests are arriving. I really don't want to do this. Well at least my best friend, Tyler, will be there to keep me entertained. He's hilarious.

"And now, for the lady of the hour, presenting Princess Karyn!" (Music plays)

"Thank you everyone! Thank you so much for coming to my party!" That's what my parents tell me to say every year.

(All the guests are seated for dinner. Karyn twirls her pasta with a bored look on her face)

"Hey, I got a surprise for you," whispers Tyler.

"Well whatever it is, I hope it's better than this!"

"I'm going to sneak out. Wait a few minutes and meet me on the terrace"

"Oh yea!", whispered Karyn.

(Tyler exits. Karyn exits shortly after)

"Hey! So what's the surprise?..... OMG!!! BURGERS!!!! You're the best!!!!" screamed Karyn.

Karyn and Tyler sat on the ground in their formal dress and tux enjoying a nice juicy burger!

- You don't have to be an expert to start cooking. It's easier than you may think!-

Rainbow Spaghetti

Ingredients

- 1 package of Spaghetti pasta
- Various Food Colorings

Tools

- Tablespoon
- Large Pot
- Strainer/Colander
- Freezer bags (Qty per number of food colorings)

Instructions

1. Boil spaghetti noodles until done. (Do not overcook)

2. While spaghetti is boiling, place 2 tablespoons of water mixed with about 20 drops of food coloring in separate freezer bags.

3. Drain water from spaghetti, and rinse with cold water.

4. Evenly divide pasta into freezer bags, and seal.

5. Let each bag sit for 2 minutes.

6. Separately drain each bag in strainer, and rinse with cold water.

7. Mix all spaghetti in a pot or serving bowl.

Homemade Nachos

Ingredients

- Whole Grain Tortilla Chips
- Block Cheddar Cheese
- Chopped Spinach
- 1 pound Breakfast Sausage
- ¼ cup - 2% Milk
- 1 can of Diced Tomatoes & Green Chiles
- ¼ cup of Chicken Broth

Directions:

1. Heat large skillet to brown sausage. Drain grease.

2. Cube Cheddar Cheese, and heat in saucepan on low heat.

3. Add can of diced tomatoes to cheese and milk to thin the cheese.

4. Steam spinach and drain water.

5. Mix spinach, cheese, and meat together.

6. Serve over tortilla chips.

Farkle Darwin was a 13 year old kid chef who loved to cook game day snacks for his family and friends. One day, Farkle was watching TV, and heard about a cooking contest that kids could enter. The grand prize would be to cook a Super Bowl dish for the President of the United States and the first family! Farkle was so excited, he immediately asked his mom to let him enter his Game Day Nachos. She agreed, and he won!!! Farkle was chosen to cook nachos for the President at the white house. Farkle knew that he couldn't just make any type of plain nachos because it was the President that he was going to be cooking for.

He looked at every website he could to find the perfect type of Nachos. Finally, Farkle figured out that he should create his very own homemade nachos, but this time, he would make them healthier by adding spinach. Everybody who had tasted his nachos was impressed. Farkle got all of his special ingredients, packed his mom's car, and took off to the white house.

Once Farkle arrived, he could not believe that he was actually there. Also, the white house was the biggest house he had ever seen in his entire life. He asked the bodyguards who were standing in front to help him carry all of his cooking supplies to the kitchen. When he stepped inside the house, the President and his family surprised Farkle and his mom. He was super happy and started cooking. Farkle was almost done in less than one hour, but he had to decorate the plate a bit and jazz it up for the President. When Farkle served his dish to the First Family, before they even tasted the nachos, they complemented him on how decorative it looked. They ate with delight and had smiles on their faces whenever they took a bite. Farkle was so happy that the First Family adored his food that he started his own business in cooking for everyone in the city. "Chef Farkle...yea I like the sound of that!"

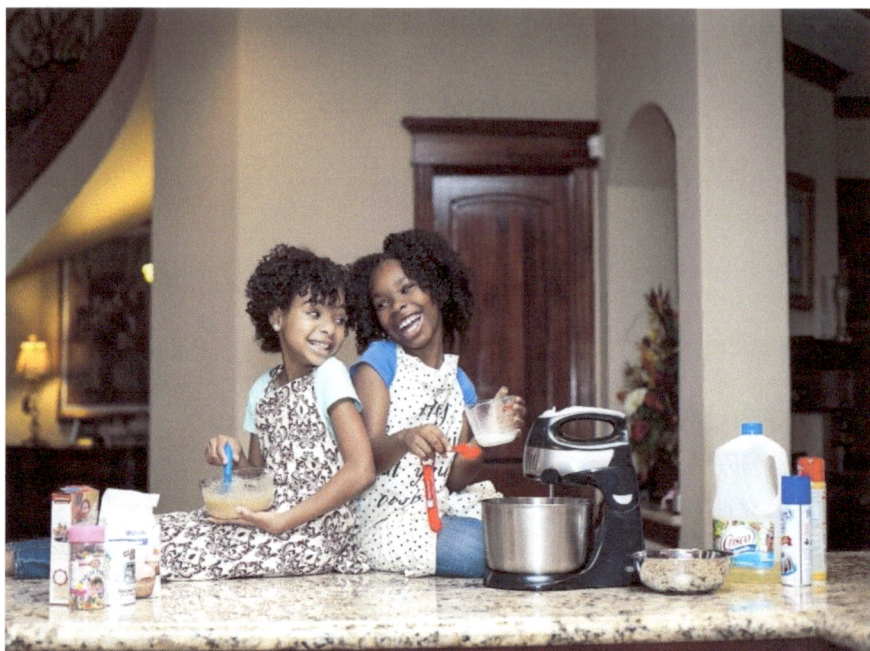

The BEST friendships
are made over a
MEAL!

☺ ☺ ☺ ☺

DESSERTS

Rainbow Sugar Cookies

Ingredients (25 cookies)

- 3 ½ cups Flour
- 1 tsp. Baking Powder
- 1 ½ (3 sticks) cups Butter, softened
- 1 cup Sugar
- 1 Egg
- 1 tsp. Vanilla
- Various flavors of Gelatin

Tools

- Cookie sheet
- Fork or cup
- Mixing spoon or electric mixer

Instructions

1. Preheat oven to 350°F.

2. Beat butter until it is creamy.

3. Mix egg, vanilla, and sugar.

4. Gradually blend in flour and baking powder.

5. Divide the cookie dough mixture per the number of gelatin flavors.

6. Knead in 2 tablespoons of gelatin onto each section of cookie dough.

7. Roll dough into 1-inch balls.

8. Roll in the extra gelatin from the packets if desired.

9. Place on a greased and floured baking sheet

10. Flatten into cookies with a fork or bottom of a cup.

11. Bake 6-8 minutes @ 350°.

12. Cool for 2 minutes on the baking sheets, and then transfer to wax paper to finish cooling.

Mug Cakes

Ingredients:

- Microwave safe mug
- Cake mix (3 tbsp.)
- Water (2tbsp.)

Directions:

- Mix all ingredients.
- Heat mixed ingredients in microwave for 2 minutes.

One day there was a girl named Peyton who entered a food contest. She wanted to make something that nobody had heard of, especially the judges. Once Peyton got home she wrote down ideas of what she could make. Then one perfect idea came to mind. She started baking her secret recipe, and would not tell anybody what she was making. Before Peyton made more of her recipe, she tasted it, and of course, it was delicious! The day of her contest, she came in feeling very confident. Everybody else's food looked familiar, but not Peyton's. Once the judges tasted all the food, they announced the winner. Peyton! Her spectacular mug cakes stole the show.

Edible Glitter

Ingredients

- ¼ cup of sugar
- ½ teaspoon for food coloring (various colors)

Tools

- Oven safe bowl

Instructions

1. Preheat oven to 350° F.

2. Mix sugar with food coloring.

3. Bake 10 minutes at 350°F.

4. Let cool.

Fruit Pizza Supreme

Ingredients

- 1 pkg. (8 oz.) softened Cream Cheese
- 1 pkg. (16.5 oz.) refrigerated sliceable sugar cookies
- ¼ cup sugar
- ½ tsp. vanilla
- 4 cups of your favorite fresh fruit
- ¼ cup apricot preserves
- 1 tbsp. water

Directions

1. Preheat oven to 375°F.
2. Line 12-inch pizza pan with foil, and spray with cooking spray.
3. Arrange cookie dough slices in single layer in prepared pan, and press together to completely cover bottom of pan.
4. Bake 14 minutes, and let cool completely.
5. Invert onto plate; carefully remove foil. Turn crust over; place on plate.
6. Beat cream cheese, sugar and vanilla with mixer until blended.
7. Spread cream mix onto crust.
8. Top with your favorite fruit.

9. Mix preserves and water; brush onto fruit.

10. Refrigerate fruit pizza for 2 hours.

Don't Blow My House Down

Ding Dong (rings the doorbell).

Rachel looks out the window and turns to her sisters and brothers and shouts, "Oh no, here comes Wolfie the wolf again!"

"Let me in, Let me in! I really want to eat some of that yummy dinner that I smell. I can smell it all the way in the forest", said Wolfie.

Rachel had a flashback to the last time that she saw Wolfie. He wasn't very nice and would do anything to eat our food. He blew part of her house down because she wouldn't let him in.

"Wolfie, calm down! I will share some of the dinner that I cooked with you if you will promise to be nice and patient," replied Rachel.

Rachel slightly cracked the door.

"Noooooooooo!", yelled Rachel's sisters. "He is going to eat everything!"

Rachel looked out of the crack and saw that Wolfie was very sad and alone. He appeared very hungry and she just couldn't leave him there.

Rachel whispered, "Do you promise to be nice?"

Wolfie replied back, "Yes, I promise and I'm sorry for how I behaved in the past."

Rachel let Wolfie in and hoped she hadn't made a mistake. She knew her siblings would be upset if anything crazy happened.

Rachel's brother pulled up a chair for Wolfie and everyone sat down and ate together at once.

Wolfie jumped up and said, "This is the best food that I've had in a very long time. Since everyone has been so kind to let me eat dinner here, I would like to prepare my favorite dessert for everyone.

"Yay dessert!!" shouted everyone.

"I see that you have all of the ingredients. I am going to make my famous banana pudding." said Wolfie.

Banana Pudding Supreme

Ingredients

- 1/3 cup all-purpose flour
- Dash of salt
- 2 ½ cups 1% low-fat milk
- 1 (14-oz.) can fat-free sweetened condensed milk
- 2 egg yolks, lightly beaten
- 2 teaspoons vanilla extract
- 3 cups sliced ripe bananas
- 48 reduced-fat vanilla wafers
- 4 egg whites
- ¼ cup sugar

Directions

1. Preheat oven to 325°. Combine flour and salt in a medium saucepan. Gradually stir in 1% milk, sweetened condensed milk, and yolks, and cook over medium heat, stirring constantly, 8 to 10 minutes or until thickened. Remove from heat; stir in vanilla.

2. Layer 3 banana slices, 3 ½ Tbsp. pudding, and 3 vanilla wafers in each of 8 (1-cup) ramekins or ovenproof glass

dishes. Top each with 6 banana slices, 3 ½ Tbsp. pudding, and 3 vanilla wafers.

3. Beat egg whites at high speed with an electric mixer until foamy. Add sugar, 1 Tbsp. at a time, beating until stiff peaks form and sugar dissolves (2 to 4 minutes). Spread about ½ cup meringue over each pudding.

4. Bake at 325° for 15 to 20 minutes or until golden. Let cool 30 minutes.

Drinks

Samantha's Party

"There are just a few hours to party time!" Samantha had been at her school for just one semester, and was adjusting to making new friends. She asked her mom and dad if she could have a small gathering with several of her classmates. Her parents agreed and helped her prepare snacks. They also help setup board games to play. "I feel like something is missing", thought Samantha.

Samantha checked the games. "I want my new friends to have fun while they are here. I hope they like my choice of games" Samantha looked over her game room and she had a station for checkers, monopoly, Uno, and Xbox. "Everything is ready to go, but there is still something missing."

Samantha checked the snack table. "I want my new friends to enjoy the food that me and my parents prepared." Samantha looked over the snack table and double checked her snacks. "Everything is ready to go, but I still feel like there is still something missing."

"Well, everyone will start arriving within the next 30 minutes. I'm so excited and so nervous."

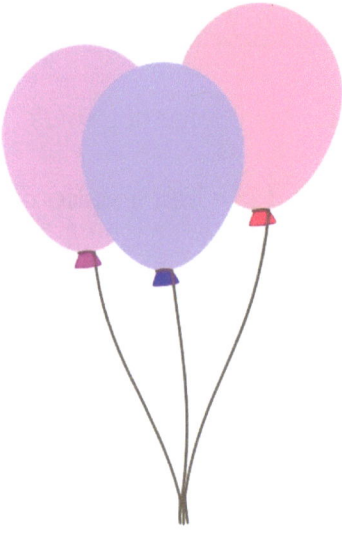

Samantha gasped, "I know what's missing! I have games and food but I don't have any drinks prepared!! Samantha wanted everything to be perfect so she wanted to make something special. She raced to the kitchen and began to search around for ingredients. "What can I make in such little time?" Samantha's mom walked into the kitchen and found her daughter frantically scrambling around. "Sammy, what are you looking for?, asked Samantha's mom.

"Mom, I want to make a punch for my friends. I totally forgot about drinks." replied Samantha. "Its fine, Samantha, I have the perfect idea….you and your friends will love it". Samantha's mom goes into the freezer and takes out a pint of raspberry sherbet. "Mom, we don't have time for this. I need drinks, not sherbet!", Samantha stated. "Be patient, Sammy and pay attention."

Samantha's mom took a punch bowl and emptied the sherbet into the bowl. She opened and poured a can of pineapple juice into the bowl. She then poured sprite (ginger ale) into the mixture. Samantha had never seen her mom prepare this before so she was quite amazed. "Mom, may I try it?" "Of course, Sam. Tell me if I need to add anything," said mom. "Mom, this is excellent! I love it and my friends will also." *(Doorbell Rings) Samantha's Dad opens the door and lets the guests inside.*

"Hi everyone. I'm glad you all could come. Let's have fun!!!!" The gathering was a hit and all of Samantha's friends loved the Sherbet punch.

Fruit Smoothie

Ingredients

- 1 banana
- 6 strawberries
- 1 kiwi
- ½ cup vanilla frozen yogurt
- ¾ cup pineapple and orange
- Ice

Tools

- Blender

Directions

1. Add 1 cup of ice to blender.
2. Clean fresh fruit.
3. Add all ingredients to ice in the blender.
4. Turn blender on medium speed.

Your smoothie is served!!!!!!

Fresh Grape Juice

Ingredients

- 1 lb. Ripe purple grapes
- Boiling water (2 cups)
- ½ cup of sugar

Tools

- Blender
- Mason jar

Directions:

1. Rinse Grapes.

2. Mix grapes and water into a blender.

3. Add sugar or sugar substitute.

4. Store juice mixture in a Mason jar to stay fresh.

5. Place in refrigerator.

Healthy Strawberry Lemonade Slurpee

Ingredients (Makes 3-4 glasses)

- 2 cups of fresh squeezed lemon juice or lemonade
- 1- ½ cups of ice
- ½ cup of frozen strawberries

Fruit Alternatives

- Mango
- Pineapple
- Blueberries
- Peaches
- Raspberries
- Banana
- Or any frozen fruit flavor

Tools

- Blender

Instructions

1. Rinse fruit and cut into slices, if necessary.

2. Blend fruit, lemonade, and ice in blender.

3. Serve.

Kamryn and Saniya Give Back

It was almost the holiday season. The Thanksgiving and Christmas holidays were around the corner, so that also meant that Christmas break was coming soon. Kamryn and Saniya were very excited because the holiday season meant that they could see their family, eat great food, and get gifts.

Kamryn and Saniya were riding the school bus home, and began to think about the season and how much fun they planned to have during their break.

"What are you asking your parents to get you for Christmas?" Saniya asked Kamryn.

Kamryn said, " I really want a new computer. What about you, Saniya?"

"I want my mom to get me a new iPod", said Saniya.

"That sounds cool," replied Kamryn.

Suddenly the bus stopped at a redlight. The girls looked out of the window and saw a family with two kids sleeping on the sidewalk.

They instantly got sad.

"I wish we could do something for them," said Saniya.

Kamryn replied, " I know, we are so blessed and they don't have anythng."

"Maybe we can ask our parents if we can make them a dinner, said Saniya.

That's an awesome idea, said Kamryn.

Let's prepare a menu for them, said Saniya.

The girls took a tablet out of their backpack and began to plan what they could prepare for the family that they saw outside.

"Well here is our stop, let's go", said Saniya.

Both of the girls got off the bus and departed to their homes.

"Hey mom", Saniya said.

"Hi honey, how was your ride home?, Saniya's mom asked.

"Well, it was great until Kamryn and I saw a homeless family living on the streets. Since the holidays are coming up, Kamryn and I thought that we could show them how much God cares about them by cooking a feast and donating presents. Maybe we can call it "Kam and Niya Give Back."

 Ring, ring, ring! The telephone in Saniya's home begins ringing.

Saniya's mom answered the phone, "Hello."

"Hi, this is Kamryn's mom. How are you?"

"Im fine and you", replied Saniya's mom.

"Good, thank you for asking. Kamryn's just arrived home and told me that she and Saniya wanted to do something special for homeless families for the holidays. I think this is great idea." – Kamryn's mom.

"Yes, Saniya just mentioned that too, so maybe we can help the girls prepare a meal to feed the homeless family."

Kamryn and Saniya fixed a fabulous feast with the help of their moms. They both learned a valuable lesson about compassion. It is more rewarding to give than to receive, and the girls realized how many families didn't have the things they needed like food. Kamryn and Saniya realized how fortunate they both are and decided to worry less about begging their parents for gifts, and more about giving back.

www.ingramcontent.com/pod-product-compliance
Lightning Source LLC
LaVergne TN
LVHW010028070426
835513LV00001B/7